The Young Scientist Investigates

Water

by
Terry Jennings

 CHILDRENS PRESS ®
CHICAGO

Illustrated by
John Barber
Norma Burgin
Karen Daws
Gary Hincks
Tony Morris
Tudor Artists

———————————————

Library of Congress Cataloging-in-Publication Data

Jennings, Terry J.
    Water / by Terry Jennings.
        p.   cm. — (The Young scientist investigates.)
    Includes index.
    Summary: An introduction to the study of water and its
properties, origins, and uses. Includes study questions, activities,
and experiments.
    ISBN 0-516-08410-0
    1. Water—Juvenile literature. [1. Water.] I. Title. II. Series:
Jennings, Terry J. Young scientist investigates.
GB662.3.J45   1988
553.7—dc 19   88-22871
                                                              CIP
                                                              AC

North American edition published in 1989 by Regensteiner
Publishing Enterprises, Inc.

© Terry Jennings 1982
First published 1982 by Oxford University Press

Printed in the United States of America
1 2 3 4 5 6 7 8 9 10 R 98 97 96 95 94 93 92 91 90 89

The Young Scientist Investigates
Water

Contents

Water everywhere

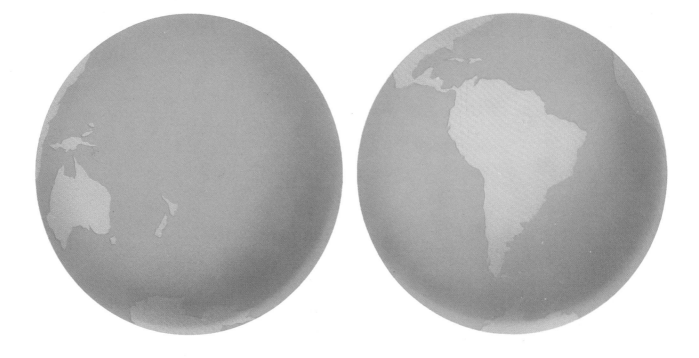

Most of the world is covered by water. Nearly three-quarters of the surface of the world is covered by oceans and seas. The water in the sea is salty. There is also a lot of water on the land. There is water in ponds, streams, rivers, lakes, and in the soil. This water comes from rain. It is not salty. There is a lot of water in our bodies. There is a lot of water in all animals and plants. Without water everything would die.

Plants and animals that live in the sea have water all around them. But the animals that live on the land cannot drink sea water because it is salty. These animals drink water from ponds, lakes, rivers, and streams. Plants that live on the land take in water from the soil through their roots.

What we use water for

Our bodies contain a lot of water. We also use fresh water in many ways. We drink water or other liquids that are mostly water. We use water for getting rid of our waste materials.

We use water to keep ourselves clean. Water is needed for cooking and washing. It also is used for cleaning clothes, cars, walls, and floors. We use water for pleasure when we swim, sail, or water ski.

Using water to cool molten copper

In places where there is plenty of water, each person uses between 39½ and 132 gallons a day. Factories and power plants also use lots of water. All of this water has to be collected from rainfall or pumped out of rivers, lakes, and wells. There is plenty of water in the sea, but it is difficult and expensive to get the salt out of it. In many dry parts of the world, people have to make do with very little water.

An oasis in the desert

Cleaning the body of a new car before it is painted

Water being used in a paper mill

Clean water

When it rains some of the water soaks into the ground. If you dig deep enough you will find water. Some people get their water from wells. A well is a hole dug in the ground. In places water bubbles out of the ground. Where the water comes out of the ground is called a spring. Many rivers start from springs. The rivers get bigger as more water goes into them from other springs and streams.

The water in a river is always moving. The water flows downhill towards the sea. Most of the water we use comes from rivers. The water is kept in big lakes called reservoirs. Water is stored in the reservoirs until it is needed. Then the water goes down a pipe to the filtration plant. At the filtration plant the water is made clean.

The water soaks through beds of sand and gravel. The dirt stays behind in the sand and gravel. Then a gas called chlorine is put into the water to kill any germs. The clean water goes along big pipes under the roads. The pipes take clean water to the taps in our homes.

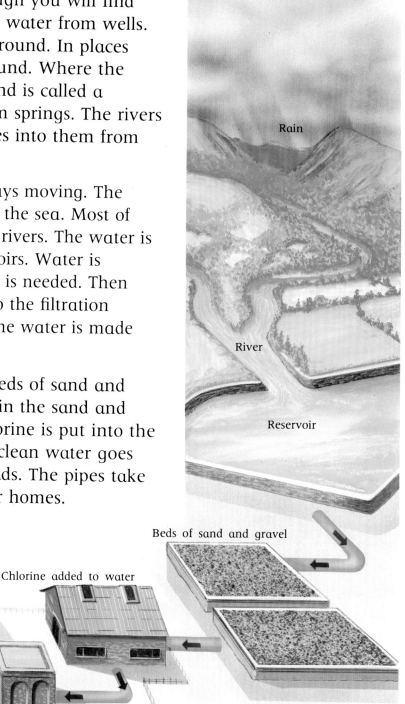

Rain

River

Reservoir

Filtration plant

Water tower

Chlorine added to water

Beds of sand and gravel

Houses

Pump house

6

Dirty water

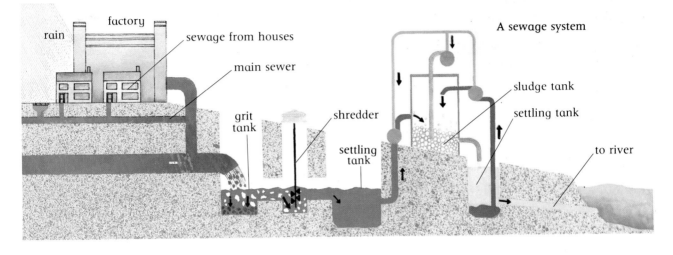

rain

factory

sewage from houses

main sewer

A sewage system

grit tank

shredder

sludge tank

settling tank

settling tank

to river

Dirty water being pumped through layers of gravel at a sewage system

A polluted river

Dirty water from our houses goes down the drain. From the drain the water goes along a large pipe called a sewer to the sewage system. At the sewage system the dirty water is put into big tanks. Some of the dirt sinks to the bottom of the tanks. Then the water passes through layers of sand or gravel. More of the dirt sticks to the sand or gravel. The water is now clean enough to go into a river. It is not clean enough to drink, though.

Many towns and factories are built by lakes and rivers so that they can use the water. But some of these towns and factories do not clean the water before they put it back in the rivers and lakes. The water may even contain poisonous substances. This dirtying of water (and air) is called pollution. Pollution makes rivers and lakes smell. It kills water plants and animals. It makes the water unfit for human use. Even the sea becomes polluted by the substances dumped in rivers. The sea is also polluted by oil and other substances from ships.

Ice and steam

When it is very cold, water freezes and turns solid. The water becomes ice. Ice is lighter than water. If you put a piece of ice into water, the ice will float. In cold parts of the world, huge pieces of ice float in the sea. These giant pieces of ice are called icebergs. In some cold countries there are also great rivers of ice on the land. These are called glaciers.

When water is heated it turns to vapor. The water disappears into the air. We say the water has *evaporated*. When vapor cools it turns back to water.

Vapor from a boiling kettle turns back to drops of water that float in the air. We call these tiny drops of water, that float in the air, steam. Clouds, fog, and mist are like steam. They are made of millions of little drops of water that float in the air.

Cooling a drink with ice cubes

A glacier

A boiling kettle

An iceberg

Clouds, rain, fog, and snow

Water vapor

A misty day

A snowflake

All over the world water is turning to vapor. The sun shining on the sea turns a lot of water to water vapor all the time. The seawater evaporates and forms water vapor. The water vapor disappears into the air. High in the sky it is cold, and the water vapor cools to form clouds. The millions of tiny drops of water that make a cloud are so small and light that they float in the air. If they are cooled still more, the tiny drops of water join together. The big drops that are formed are too heavy to float in the air. They fall to the ground as rain.

Clouds may be formed right down near the ground. Then we have mist or fog. You can see the tiny drops of water on your clothes if you go for a walk when it is misty or foggy.

When the weather is very cold, the tiny drops of water in the clouds may turn to ice. Each little piece of ice forms a shape called a crystal. The ice crystals grow bigger and fall as snowflakes. Snowflakes form very beautiful patterns.

9

Dew and ice

Often in the winter we wake up to find the ground covered with frost. The white powder we call frost is, of course, ice. The water that made the frost was in the air. When the air is warm we do not notice the water vapor in it. But at night when the air gets colder, even in summer, it can no longer hold as much water vapor. So some of the vapor settles on the grass, leaves, and stones and forms small drops of water. This is called dew.

A frosty scene

If the air is very cold, as it often is in winter, then the tiny drops of dew freeze to form frost. In cold weather ice may form on wet roads and puddles. This ice is dangerous to traffic as it may cause accidents. The surface of water always freezes first. It is a good thing for water animals and plants that ice forms on top of the water. If ice formed at the bottom the plants and animals would be frozen to death.

Dew

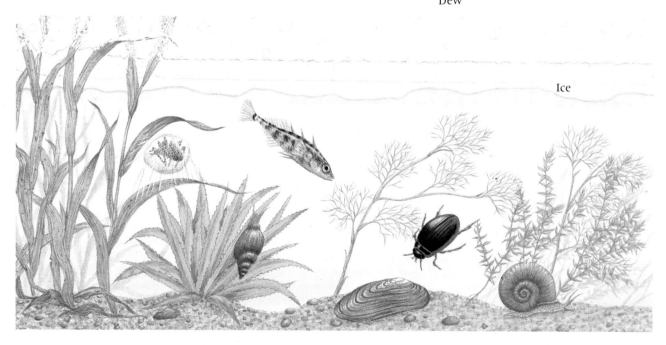
Ice

Where our water comes from

Planting trees in the desert

A well in the desert

We have only a certain amount of water on the Earth. The sun shines on the sea and lots of water vapor goes into the air. When the water vapor cools it falls as rain or snow. Much of the rain or melted snow goes into rivers and streams. Rivers and streams flow into the sea. So we are using the same water over and over again. Many people in the world do not have enough water to drink or for growing their food. They live in areas where little rain falls.

In such dry lands, farmers use water from rivers or wells to make their crops grow. The water is pumped into ditches through the fields. These ditches make the ground moist. So the crops grow better. People can live only where they can get water. In some parts of Africa and India, people have to walk many miles to get water from a well or river. We are lucky to live in a country where there is enough rainfall and fresh clean water. But we must not waste the water we do have.

Using water to make crops grow in the desert

Do you remember?

(Look for the answers in the part of the book you have just been reading if you do not know them.)

1 How much of the surface of the Earth is covered by oceans and seas?

2 How is seawater different from rain water?

3 What are some of the things we use water for?

4 Where there is plenty of water, how much may each person use in a day?

5 How do rivers start?

6 Where does most of the water we use in our homes come from?

7 What is a reservoir?

8 How does the filtration plant make our water clean and fit to drink?

9 What happens if dirty water from towns and factories is put straight into rivers?

10 How does the sewage system get most of the dirt out of the water?

11 What is pollution and what does it do to water?

12 How does the sea become polluted?

13 What happens to water when it is very cold?

14 What does water turn into when it is heated?

15 What do we say has happened when water disappears into the air?

16 What are steam, clouds, fog, and mist made from?

17 What often happens when clouds are cooled?

18 What are snowflakes made of and what do they look like?

19 Where does the ice first form on a pond in winter?

20 Why should we not waste water?

Things to do

1 **Pretend you are a spaceman.** You are on a visit to this country from Mars. You see water for the very first time. Write a letter to your friends on Mars telling them what water is like.

2 **How much do animals drink?** Do you have a pet at home? Do you give it clean water each day? How much does it drink each day? How much water and other liquids do you drink in a day? Keep a note of all the cups of milk, lemonade, juice, tea, and other drinks you have in a day. How many quarts do these add up to?

3 Find out as much as you can about the water supply where you live. Make a wallchart about it. Include on the wallchart a plan of your house, showing the position of the water taps, sinks, baths, showers, toilets, hot-water boilers, radiators, etc.

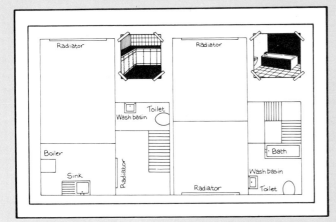

4 Make a river wallchart. Collect pictures of rivers, boats, bridges, river fish, river plants, and anything else to do with rivers. Make wallcharts or a book with your pictures.

5 Find out about water pressure. Push a plastic funnel into each end of a piece of plastic or rubber tubing. Hold the two funnels side by side. Ask a friend to pour

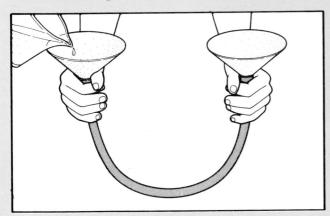

water into one of the funnels. What happens to the other funnel? Is there water in it? Is there water in the tube?

Now hold one funnel up above the other. What happens to the water level in the funnels? Lower the funnels. What happens to the water level?

Make a hole near the bottom of a plastic bottle with a large nail. Push the end of the rubber or plastic tubing into the hole. Make a good tight fit. Seal any gaps with clay. Push the end of an old ball-point pen into the free end of the tube.

Fill the bottle with water. The water comes out of the end of the rubber tube like a fountain. The higher you raise the bottle above the end of the tube, the higher the fountain rises because there is more pressure.

In a similar way, water is pumped from the reservoir to a high water tower. Then the water runs, under pressure, from the tower to the taps in our houses.

6 Find some poems about rain. Copy them into your notebook. Try writing a little poem of your own about rain. Ask some friends to help you write some music to go with your poem. Write your music down if you can.

7 Breathe on a window pane or a mirror. What happens? Rub your finger on it. What do you find?

8 Find out about water in the air. Take the label off an empty cocoa or coffee tin or a can that has held vegetables or fruit. Carefully wash out the tin until it is clean.

Ice cubes

Fill the tin with ice cubes. Leave the tin in the room for a little while. Then look at the outside of the tin. Feel it. What has happened on the outside of the tin? Why?

Try this on a dry day and again on a wet day. Does the weather make any difference to what happens?

9 Collect pictures of the various kinds of clouds. What kinds of weather do we get when the different types of cloud are in the sky?

10 *Carefully* hold a cold spoon near the spout of a kettle of boiling water. See how the little drops of water collect together to form larger drops that begin to fall like rain. Something similar to this happens in a cloud when raindrops form.

11 Discover what happens when water freezes. Fill a small plastic bottle (not a glass one) to the top with water. Tightly screw on the stopper. Fill a bowl with ice cubes and sprinkle some salt over them.

Small plastic bottle filled with water

Ice cubes

Push the bottle of water under the ice cubes. Leave it there for about an hour.

Instead of using ice cubes, you could, if you are able to, put a small plastic bottle of water in the freezing compartment of the refrigerator overnight.

Look at the bottle when the water has frozen. What has happened to the bottle? Do you now know why the water pipes sometimes burst in very cold weather? Why is the damage not noticed until the warmer weather comes?

14

12 Find out more about water pressure. Take a tall plastic bottle, and with a large nail make holes in it similar to those in the picture.

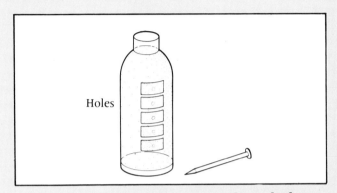

Holes

Stand the bottle near the sink and plug the holes with sticky tape or clay. Fill the bottle with water. When the plugs are removed, water will flow out of the holes. From which holes does the strongest jet of water flow? Write a sentence to explain what happens. Use these three words in the sentence: depth, pressure, increases.

Can you see now why deep-sea divers have to wear special suits?

13 Find out about melting snow. Fill a jar with snow or pieces of ice. See how much water is formed when it melts. Sprinkle some salt on snow or ice and see what happens. When do workmen do this?

Snow

Salt

14 Make a simple rain gauge. Stand it out in the open away from trees and buildings. Use the rain gauge to find out how much rain has fallen each day. Measure the depth of water in inches.

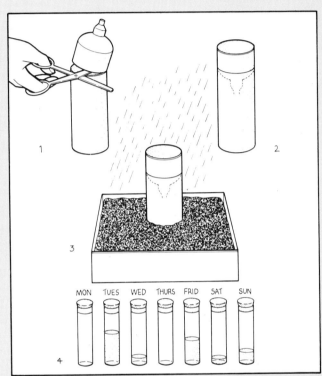

1

2

3

4

MON TUES WED THURS FRID SAT SUN

15 Pretend you are walking through a forest. Suddenly there is a bad thunderstorm. Write a story about your adventures.

16 Make a model snow scene. Include a snowman in your scene. What will you use to represent the snow?

Water at work

We use water to do many things for us. Some people use water to heat their homes. The water is heated in a boiler. Hot water from the boiler goes along pipes to radiators. The hot radiators warm the air in the room. After the water has been through the radiators it is cool. So it goes back to the boiler to be heated again. We also use water to cool things. Motor cars and trucks have radiators. But these radiators have cold water in them. The water is used to take away heat from the engine so that the engine does not get too hot.

Water is used at some power stations to make electricity. These power stations are called hydroelectric power stations. A hydroelectric power station has a dam. Big pipes carry water to large waterwheels below the dam. These waterwheels are called turbines. The water rushes down the pipes and turns the turbines very quickly. The turbines drive the generators that make electricity. The electricity goes along wires to houses and factories.

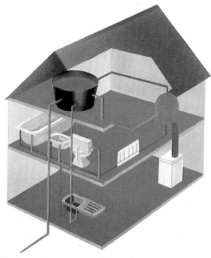
Hot water system in a house

Car radiator

How a hydroelectric power plant works

Hydroelectric power plant

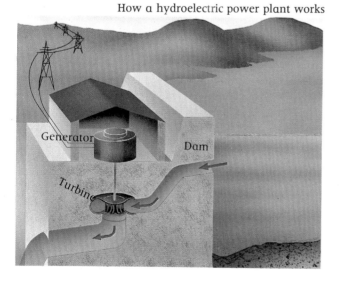
Generator
Dam
Turbine

Evaporating

Wet clothes hung out on a sunny day soon dry. Puddles on the playground and roads soon dry up when the sun comes out. The water turns to vapor and disappears into the air. The water has evaporated. Wet clothes and puddles will also dry on a cloudy day. But they dry faster when the sun is shining.

Heat makes water evaporate quickly. When a kettle of water is heated, some of the water evaporates. This water turns into vapor. Vapor from a boiling kettle cools to form little drops of water that float in the air. These little drops of water form steam. We cannot see the water vapor but we can see the steam.

Water can be a liquid like that which comes out of the tap. If we warm water it turns into the gas called water vapor. When water vapor is cooled, it turns back to water. If we cool water it becomes solid ice. When ice is warmed it turns back to water. So, water can be a solid, a liquid, or a gas.

ice cube   water   steam

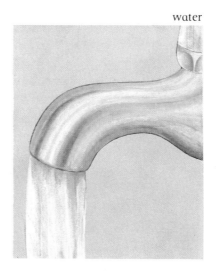

Wet and dry

Water makes things wet. If you wear wool or cotton clothes out in the rain they will get very wet. But some materials are not easy to wet right through. The materials from which tents, raincoats, and umbrellas are made do not let water through. We say these materials are waterproof.

Some birds and other animals have waterproof coverings. Many ducks dive under water to find food. When they come to the surface again, they shake their feathers and the water runs off them. The water also shakes off the fur of seals and otters.

Duck

Seal

Otter

Washing hands in cold water

Washing hands in cold, soapy water

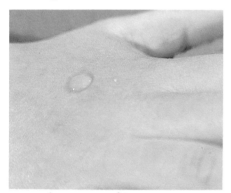

Drop of water on skin

Drying hair with a towel

Have you ever tried to wash your hands in cold water? The water will not wet your hands very well. The water forms large drops that run off your skin leaving it dry. This is because your skin has an oily layer that waterproofs it. If you wash your hands with soapy water, you can wet them all over.

Soap makes the water spread more easily. Sometimes it is useful to have materials that wet easily. Blotting paper soaks up ink, water, and other liquids. So does a sponge or towel. These are useful for drying things.

Blotting paper

Ink

Dissolving things

If you put a spoonful of sugar in a jar of water, the sugar soon disappears. We have made a sugar *solution*. The sugar disappears even quicker if the water is warm. A spoonful of salt also disappears when it is put in a jar of water. We say that when the sugar and salt disappear in water, they have dissolved.

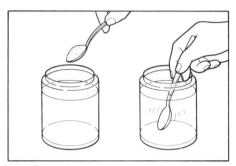
Dissolving sugar in water

Water will dissolve many things. Rainwater and streams will even dissolve some rocks. In areas where the hills are made of limestone, the streams have dissolved away much rock. Seawater is a salt solution. The salt has come from rocks the water has flowed over.

Stream dissolving away rock to form a deep valley (gorge)

A limestone gorge

Boiling water in a saucepan

Water also dissolves air. Fishes and many other water animals obtain the oxygen they breathe from the air that has been dissolved in the water. You can see this air that was dissolved if you heat water in a saucepan. The air comes off in bubbles. If you leave a saucer of sugar or salt solution on a radiator, the water will soon evaporate . The sugar or salt will be left on the saucer.

Floating and sinking

Many things will float in water. Boats and ships float in water. They are streamlined so that they cut through the water easily. The first boats were made of wood. Nowadays large ships are made of steel. Large ships can cross the world's oceans and seas. They carry people and cargoes from one country to another.

An old wooden sailing ship

A harbor scene

Much of our food is brought in ships from other countries. Many ships carry their cargoes in large containers. At the port these containers can be lifted by crane straight onto trucks or railway wagons. The containers are then taken to where they are needed. Ships also travel on big rivers.

A container ship

A canal barge

Sometimes people dig large trenches between towns. These trenches are filled with water. They are called canals. The long, narrow boats that travel on canals are called barges. Barges carry heavy things such as rocks for roadmaking and coal. Several barges often travel together pulled by one barge that has an engine.

Living in dry places

Camel

Gerboa

Very few plants and animals can live in the deserts of the world. This is because there is so little water. Camels can make long journeys across the desert. But a camel still has to drink. It drinks as much as 34⅓ gallons of water at a time. The camel can live on this water for up to three weeks.

A gerboa is a small desert animal that is sometimes called a desert rat. A gerboa never drinks. It gets the little water it needs from seeds, roots, and the other pieces of plants it eats.

A cactus plant

Plants lose most water through their leaves. Cacti and other desert plants have their leaves turned into spines. The spines stop the cacti from being eaten by animals and also catch little drops of dew. Cacti have very long roots that spread out to collect any rain or dew from a large area. A cactus can live for a long time without water. When it does rain, the cactus takes up water and stores it in its large stem. The water is then used up very slowly.

Camels in the desert

Cacti in the desert

22

Living in the water

Water lilies

Water lilies grow in still water. The large leaves and flowers of water lilies float on the surface of the water. The leaves of many plants that grow underwater in fast flowing rivers are long and narrow. They bend and sway with the current. If the leaves were wide they would be swept away.

Plants growing in fast-flowing river

The seaweed that grows in the sea is also narrow so that it does not get swept away by the waves. The seaweed is firmly fixed to rocks. Animals that live in the water and that move fast are streamlined. They have a smooth and slim shape so that the water flows by them easily.

Seaweeds

Fishes, dolphins, and porpoises all have a streamlined shape. Some small animals that live in still water are able to run on top of the water. The pond strider is able to do this.

A pike

A pond strider

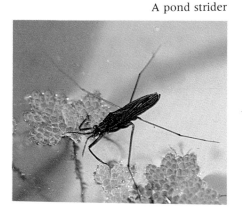

The sea

Most of the world is covered by oceans and seas. The bottom of the sea is not flat like the seashore. There are mountains, deep valleys, and even volcanoes under the sea. The sea is always moving. Twice each day the level of the water rises. The sea covers the shore and waves crash against the rocks. We say that the tide is in.

High tide

Twice each day the level of the sea falls. The seashore is uncovered and the tide has gone out. When the tide goes out, some animals including fishes, sea urchins, and starfish are left in the pools. A few animals, such as cockles, razor shells, and some crabs bury themselves in wet mud or sand. Some other animals, such as limpets, barnacles, winkles, and sea anemones cling to the rocks. They all wait until the tide comes back in again.

Low tide

Mountains, valleys, and volcanoes under the sea

A rock pool at low tide.
Can you name these plants and animals?

Plankton plants and animals

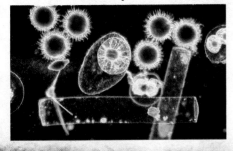

Many other plants and animals live in the sea. Lots of them are so small that you can see them only with a microscope. The tiny plants and animals are called plankton. The plankton plants and animals are eaten by larger animals such as fishes and whales.

25

Do you remember?

1 How do some people use water to heat their homes?

2 How is the water different after it has been through the radiators in a house?

3 What does a car or truck radiator do?

4 What is a hydroelectric power plant?

5 How can we make water evaporate faster?

6 What are the three different forms in which water can be found?

7 What are waterproof materials like?

8 Why is it not easy to wash your hands in cold water?

9 What does soap do to the water to help us wash our hands?

10 Why is it sometimes useful to have materials that wet easily?

11 How would you make a salt solution?

12 What do we say sugar and salt have done when we make them disappear in water?

13 How could you get the sugar back from a sugar solution?

14 Where do fishes and many other water animals get the oxygen that they breathe?

15 Why are boats and ships streamlined?

16 What do we call the long, narrow boats that sail on canals?

17 How does a cactus in the desert get its water and where is the water stored?

18 How do seaweed and plants growing in fast-flowing rivers stop themselves from being washed away?

19 What do we say has happened when twice each day the level of the sea rises and falls?

20 What are the tiny plants and animals called that live in the sea?

Things to do

1 **Find out about evaporation.** Get a saucer and a small jar. Fill the jar to the top with water. Carefully empty this water into a saucer. Stand the saucer on a windowsill or shelf indoors. Fill the jar to the top again with water.
Stand it by the side of the saucer of water. What happens to the water after a day or so? Which dries up first? Why? Where has the water gone?

2 **Make a waterwheel.** Cut the metal foil top from a yogurt carton or cream carton. Make a small neat hole in the

center. Cut 8 slits at equal distances apart around the edge. Twist the pieces between the cuts to make paddles. Push a knitting needle through the hole in the middle of the wheel.

Hold the waterwheel under a running tap. Does the wheel go around? This is how a turbine at a hydroelectric power plant is also turned.

3   Dip some pieces of old clothing and other materials in water. Make a list of those materials that get wet at once. What are they made of? Why do some clothes get wet through, while others do not?

4   Look at drops of water. Dip the point of a pencil in water. Hold the pencil point downwards. What happens to the water on the pencil? Shake the pencil gently. What happens to the drop of water? Now shake the pencil hard. What happens to the drop of water?

Shake some drops of water on the top of a table. Look at them with a magnifying glass or hand lens. Gently touch each one of the drops with the point of your pencil. What do you see? Put drops of water on all sorts of materials and surfaces: try newspaper, waxed paper, a raincoat, a handkerchief, a recently polished car (with permission!), and a car that has not been polished for a long time. What happens in each case?

If you can get one, an eye dropper is very useful for making drops of water.

5   Find out about the surface of water. Half-fill a glass with water. Look carefully with a hand lens or magnifying glass at the surface of the water where it meets the side of the glass. What do you see?

Fill the glass with water until it nearly overflows. Look carefully with a hand lens or magnifying glass at the surface of the water. Touch the surface gently with the point of a pencil. What happens? Tap the rim of the glass. What happens?

Carefully slide small coins or beads into the water in the glass one at a time. Keep watching the surface of the water. What do you see.

Take a clean sewing needle. Gently lower it onto the surface of the water. Does the needle float? If it does not, try again. What is the needle made of? Why does it float? Do you think the water might have a skin on it?

Do you remember that on page 23, we saw that some small animals, such as the pond strider, can walk on the surface of the water? Can you see now why they can do this?

When you have got the needle to float, put a tiny drop of liquid soap on the water. What happens to the needle?

6   Make some soap bubbles. Use a mixture of half liquid soap and half water. Use a straw to blow the bubbles. What colors are the bubbles? How far will they float in the air? What is the biggest bubble you can make?

Add a little glycerine to the mixture of liquid soap and water. Blow bubbles with it. Can you now make even bigger bubbles? Find out the best amount of glycerine to add to the mixture to make the biggest bubbles. Bend a piece of thin wire into a loop about the size of a quarter. Dip the loop into the bubble mixture. Take it out and blow it gently. Are bubbles formed? Do different sizes and shapes of loops make different sizes and shapes of bubbles?

7   Find out which solution washes cleanest. Cut a piece of greasy cloth into three pieces. Wash one piece in warm, clean water, one in warm, soapy water, and one in warm water containing laundry detergent. Which washes the cloth the cleanest?

Many soap manufacturers say that *their* soap washes the cleanest and whitest. Cut up a dirty piece of white cloth to see which

detergent you think washes the cleanest and whitest. Use the same amount of detergent and water in each case.

8   Try dissolving substances in water. Put ¾ to 1 inch of water into a clean glass. Taste the water.

Add one teaspoonful of salt. What happens to the salt? Now stir the water. What happens to the salt as you stir? How many teaspoonfuls of salt can you make disappear in the water? Where is the salt? Taste the water. Keep adding salt. Does it all disappear?

Leave a saucer full of salt water in a warm place for a long time. What happens to the water? Look through a hand lens or magnifying glass at what is left. What is left behind? Taste it.

Do these experiments again using sugar instead of salt.

Try to dissolve all sorts of things in water. Make a list of the things that will dissolve. Which dissolve the most easily?

Do Not Taste any of the things you put in the water except for the sugar and salt.

Experiments to try

9 Make a list of things that float and sink in water. Try various things made from wood, metal, plastic, and other materials. Try putting a large air-filled ball in water. Does it float? Push down on the ball. What do you notice?

10 Find out how water affects the weight of things. If you can obtain a spring balance, hang a lump of clay from it. How much does the clay weigh?

Now lower the lump of clay on the end of the spring balance into a jar of water. How much does the clay weigh now? Does it weigh more, less, or the same? What has happened to the level of the water in the jar?

Has the weight of the clay really changed? Now pull the clay out of the water. Does it weigh more, less, or the same? Has the weight of the clay really changed?

11 Compare pond life with life on the shore. Draw pictures of some of the plants and animals that live in or near rivers. Make a list of the animals that can be found on the seashore. Collect pictures of as many of them as you can.

12 Pretend that you live at the bottom of the sea. Some scientists once lived for several weeks in a house at the bottom of the sea. Pretend that you were one of those scientists. Write a story describing what happened to you. Do not forget to say how you obtained food and air to breathe.

Do your experiments carefuly. Write or draw what you have done and what happens. Say what you have learned. Compare your findings with those of your friends.

1 Do seeds need water to grow?

What you need: Some cotton; jam jars; mustard seeds.

What you do: Put a layer of cotton 1 to 1½ inches thick in the bottom of a jam jar. Wet the cotton with cold water. Sprinkle mustard seeds on top of the cotton. Stand the jar in a warm place.

Put a layer of cotton 1 to 1½ inches thick on the bottom of another jar. Do not wet the cotton. Sprinkle mustard seeds on top of the cotton. Stand the jar in a warm place.

Look at the seeds in both jars every day. What happens? What does this tell you about seeds and water?

Try this experiment with other kinds of seeds. Peas, radishes, and lettuce seeds are good ones to try first.

2 Leaves and water

What you need: Two similar leafy shoots; three identical narrow-necked bottles.

What you do: Fill all three bottles with water. Into one put a leafy shoot. Into a second bottle put a shoot with all the leaves removed. Leave the third bottle as it is.

See that the water level in all three bottles is exactly the same. Mark the water levels, and stand the bottles on a sunny windowsill. Which bottle loses the most water and which the least? Why?

3 Wet and dry

What you need: Some thread; a drinking straw; some paper clips; some cotton; a fresh leaf.

What you do: Tie a thread around the middle of a drinking straw. Hang the straw from a hook on a shelf in a place that is free from drafts.

Carefully tie a fresh leaf to one end of the straw. Hang paper clips from a thread tied to the other end of the straw until the straw is level.

Wait half an hour. What happens to the straw? Is it still level?

Replace the leaf with a piece of damp cotton. Balance the straw again to where it is level. What happens after a while? What has happened to both the leaf and the cotton?

4 Can we clean dirty water?

What you need: Some clean jam jars; a clean flowerpot; a sheet of paper; cotton; some clean, washed sand and gravel; soil.

What you do: Shake some soil in a jar with water. What color is the water. Leave the jar to stand for two days. What happens to the water? What happens to the soil?

Put a layer of cotton in the bottom of the flowerpot. On top of this put a layer of clean gravel about 1 to 1½ inches thick.

Cover the gravel with a layer of clean sand about 1 to 1½ inches thick. Lay a piece of paper on top of the sand. Stand the flowerpot on top of a clean jar, so that the drainage holes are over the jar.

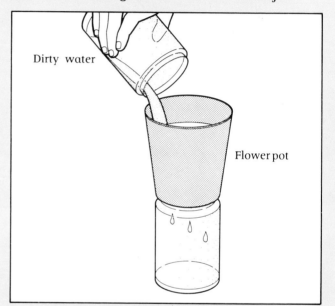

Dirty water

Flowerpot

Shake some soil up in a jar of water. Slowly and carefully pour the muddy water on to the piece of paper in the flowerpot.

What is the water like that comes out of the flowerpot into the jar at the bottom? Is it still muddy? Is it fit to drink?

Our flowerpot acts as a filter. It filters the soil out of the water. Where else is a filter used to clean dirty water? How is water made pure for drinking?

Can you use your flowerpot filter to get the salt out of salty water?

5 Floating cans

What you need: A bowl of water; an empty cocoa or coffee tin, or similar; some clay; and a marker pen.

What you do: Put the empty tin in the bowl of water. Does it float? Mark how far the water comes up the side of the tin. Mark how far the water comes up the side of the bowl.

Put a piece of clay in the tin. Does the tin float now? What has happened to the water levels?

Put more clay in the tin. How far does the water come up the side of the tin now? How far does the water come up the side of the bowl? What happens if you put still more clay in the tin?

Do this experiment again, but this time keep a record of the weight of the empty tin, and the weights of the clay you put into it. What weight of clay will the tin hold and still remain floating? What weight of clay makes the tin sink?

Try this experiment again using the same tin and the same pieces of clay. Put salt water in the bowl this time instead of tap water. What differences do you notice?

Does a ship float deeper in the water when it is carrying a heavy cargo?

6   Floating and sinking

What you need: A piece of aluminium foil; clay; a bowl of water.

What you do: Shape the piece of foil into a boat and put it on the water. Does it float? Now roll the foil tightly into a ball. Put it on the water. Does it float?

Make a clay boat that floats. Now roll the clay into a ball. Put it on the water. Does it float.

Can you understand now why ships made of steel can float?

7   Looking at the skin on water

What you need: A clean bowl; talcum powder; soapy water; 6 matchsticks; a piece of thread; a piece of cardboard or balsa wood.

What you do: Fill the bowl with water. Lightly dust the surface of the water with talcum powder. Drop onto the surface of the water one spot of soapy water. What happens? What seems to have happened to the skin on the water?

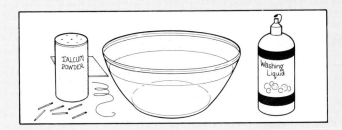

Another way of doing this experiment is to lay a loop of thread on the surface of the water or to make a ring of matchsticks. Put a spot or two of soapy water in the center of the loop of thread or ring of matchsticks. What happens?

Fill the bowl with clean water again. Make a boat shape out of cardboard or balsa wood. The boat should be about an inch long. Cut a little notch in the back of the boat. Put a small piece of soap in this. Put the boat on the water. What happens?

Glossary

Here are the meanings of some words that you might have met for the first time in this book.

Barge: a long, narrow, flat-bottomed boat.

Canal: a big trench that is filled with water and that joins towns or industrial areas.

Chlorine: a gas often added to tap water at the filtraton plant to kill any germs. Chlorine is also put in the water in swimming pools to kill germs.

Desert: a dry, treeless region of the world.

Dew: the drops of water that collect on grass, leaves, and stones when the air is too cold to hold water vapor. Dew is mainly formed at night.

Dissolve: when a substance such as salt or sugar disappears in a liquid such as water, we say it has dissolved.

Evaporate: when water is heated it disappears into the air as water vapor. We say the water has evaporated.

Hydroelectric power plant: a power plant that uses the force of running water to turn the generators that make electricity.

Icebergs: large blocks of ice that float in the sea in places where it is very cold.

Plankton: the minute plants and animals that float in seawater. Plankton is food for many fishes, whales, and other sea animals.

Pollution: the dirtying of air or water.

Reservoir: a big man-made lake in which water for drinking, making electricity, or watering fields is stored.

Sewer: a large pipe that carries dirty water.

Sewage: systems where dirty water is cleaned so that it can be put in rivers or sometimes into the sea.

Solution: when sugar disappears, or dissolves, in water, a sugar solution is formed. Many other substances will dissolve in liquids to form solutions.

Spring: where underground water comes to the surface. Many rivers start off as springs.

Steam: tiny drops of water floating in the air.

Streamlined: something that has a smooth, slim shape, so that it cuts through the water and air easily.

Tides: the rise and fall of the sea water twice each day.

Waterproof materials: materials that will not let water through.

Water vapor: the invisible gas that is formed when water is heated.

Acknowledgments

The publishers would like to thank the following for permission to reproduce transparencies:

C Alexander p. 19; Ardea p. 2, p. 7/John Daniels p. 10 (top); Barnaby's p. 17 (bottom), p. 18 (right); A Beaumont p. 8 (top); Bruce Coleman: Francisco Erize p. 8 (bottom)/Manfred Kage p. 9 (bottom)/Georgio Gualco p. 22 (left)/Jane Burton p. 23 (center left)/Hans Reinhard p. 23 (right); Colorific p. 5 (top), p. 11 (top); Courtaulds Ltd p. 5 (center left); Daily Telegraph: Audrey Stirling p. 18 (left); Robert Harding p. 10 (bottom); T Jennings p. 3 (bottom), p. 4 (center), p. 11 (bottom), p. 16 (bottom), p. 21 (top left), p. 23 (top and bottom left); Oxford Scientific Films: C C Lockwood p. 9 (top)/D H Thompson p. 22 (right)/Zig Leszczynski p. 24/Peter Parks p. 25; Picturepoint p. 5 (right), p. 11 (**center**); A Smith p. 20; A Souster p. 16 (top), p. 17 (top), p. 19 (bottom); G C Telling p. 3 (top left); Vision International: Anthea Sieveking p. 3 (top right)/Le Cossec p. 4 (left)/Anthea Sieveking p. 4 (bottom right); G Wood p. 4 (top right); ZEFA p. 5 (bottom left)/E Christian p. 21 (right)/G Mabbs p. 21 (center left)/J Schorken p. 21 (bottom left).

Illustrated by
John Barber, Norma Burgin, Karen Daws, Gary Hincks, Tony Morris and Tudor Artists.

Index